SCHIRMER'S LIBRARY
OF MUSICAL CLASSICS

Compositions for the Piano
FRÉDÉRIC CHOPIN

Edited, Revised, and Fingered by
RAFAEL JOSEFFY

Historical and Analytical Comments by
JAMES HUNEKER

<table>
<tr><td>→ BALLADES</td><td>— Library</td><td>Vol.</td><td>31</td></tr>
<tr><td>CONCERTO No. 1 IN E MINOR (Two-Piano Score) —</td><td>"</td><td>"</td><td>1350</td></tr>
<tr><td>CONCERTO No. 2 IN F MINOR (Two-Piano Score) —</td><td>"</td><td>"</td><td>1351</td></tr>
<tr><td>FOUR CONCERT-PIECES</td><td></td><td></td><td></td></tr>
<tr><td>Piano I (or Piano Solo) —</td><td>"</td><td>"</td><td>38</td></tr>
<tr><td>Piano II (reduction of orchestra accompaniment) —</td><td>"</td><td>"</td><td>1352</td></tr>
<tr><td>IMPROMPTUS —</td><td>"</td><td>"</td><td>1039</td></tr>
<tr><td>MAZURKAS —</td><td>"</td><td>"</td><td>28</td></tr>
<tr><td>NOCTURNES —</td><td>"</td><td>"</td><td>30</td></tr>
<tr><td>PRELUDES —</td><td>"</td><td>"</td><td>34</td></tr>
<tr><td>RONDOS —</td><td>"</td><td>"</td><td>1184</td></tr>
<tr><td>SCHERZI AND FANTASY —</td><td>"</td><td>"</td><td>32</td></tr>
<tr><td>MISCELLANEOUS COMPOSITIONS —</td><td>"</td><td>"</td><td>36</td></tr>
<tr><td>WALTZES —</td><td>"</td><td>"</td><td>27</td></tr>
</table>

G. SCHIRMER, Inc.

DISTRIBUTED BY
HAL•LEONARD®
CORPORATION
7777 W. BLUEMOUND RD. P.O. BOX 13819 MILWAUKEE, WI 53213

T0055351

THE BALLADES

CHOPIN composed four Ballades; the first, in G minor, opus 23, was published in June, 1836; the second, in F major-A minor, opus 38, in September, 1840; the third, in A flat, opus 47, November, 1841; and the fourth, in F minor, opus 52, in February, 1843. In his "Studies in Modern Music," W. H. Hadow has said some pertinent things about Chopin. Yet we must not unconditionally accept his statement that "in structure Chopin is a child playing with a few simple types; and almost helpless as soon as he advances beyond them; in phraseology he is a master whose felicitous perfection of style is one of the abiding treasures of the art." Chopin then, according to Hadow, is no builder of the lofty rhyme, but the poet of the single line, a maker of the phrase exquisite. This is hardly comprehensive enough. With the more classic, complex types of musical organism Chopin had little sympathy, nevertheless he contrives to write two movements of a piano sonata that are excellent—the first half of the B flat minor Sonata. But he preferred the idealized dance-forms; the Polonaise, Mazurka, and Waltz were already in existence for him to manipulate. The Ballade was not. Here he is not an imitator or remodeller, but creator. Not loosely jointed, but compact structures glowing with genius and of a definite unity in form and expression are the Ballades—commonly written in six-eight and six-four time. "None of Chopin's compositions surpasses in masterliness of form and beauty and poetry of contents his Ballades. In them he attains the acme of his power as an artist," declares Professor Niecks.

The G minor Ballade is the Odyssey of Chopin's soul; in it are the surge and thunder of the poet. That 'cello-like *Largo* with its noiseless suspension stays us for a moment at the entrance of Chopin's House Beautiful. Then, told in his most dreamy tones, the legend begins. As in some fabulous tale of the Genii this Ballade discloses surprising and delicious things. There is the tall lily in the fountain that nods to the sun. It drips in cadenced monotone and its song is echoed by the lips of the slender-hipped girl with the midnight eyes—and so I might weave a story of what I see in this Ballade and my readers would be puzzled or aghast. With such a composition any programme could be planned, even the story of the Englishman who is said to have haunted the presence of Chopin beseeching that he teach him this Ballade. That Chopin had a definite programme there can be no doubt; but, wise artist that he was he has left no clue beyond the Lithuanian poems of the Polish bard, Adam Mickiewicz. Karasowski relates that when Chopin and Schumann met in Leipsic the former confessed that he had been "incited to the creation of the Ballades by the poetry" of his fellow countryman. The true narrative tone is in this symmetrically constructed Ballade— "After Konrad Wallenrod" —the most spirited and daring work of Chopin, according to Schumann. Of the four Ballades Louis Ehlert writes: "Each one differs entirely from the others, and they have but one thing in common—their romantic working out and the nobility of their motives. Chopin relates in them, not like one who communicates something really experienced; it is as though he told what never took place, but what has sprung up in his inmost soul, the anticipation of something longed for. They may contain a strong element of national woe, much outwardly expressed and inwardly burning rage over the sufferings of his native land; yet they do not convey positive reality as does a Beethoven sonata." Which means that Chopin was not such a realist as Beethoven? Ehlert is one of the few sympathetic German commentators on Chopin, yet he did not always indicate the salient outlines of his art. Perhaps only the Slav may hope to understand Chopin thoroughly. But these Ballades are more truly touched by the universal than any of his works; they belong as much to the world as to Poland.

The G minor Ballade is a logical, well-knit and largely-planned composition; the closest parallelism may be detected in its thematic scheme. Its second theme in E flat major is lovely in line, color and sentiment. The modulating of the first theme, into A minor, and the quick answer in E major of the second, are evidences of Chopin's feeling for organic unity. Development, as in strict cyclic forms, there is not much. After the cadenza, built on a figure of wavering tonality, a waltz-like theme emerges and enjoys a capricious butterfly existence. Passage-work of an etherealized character leads to the second subject, now augmented and treated with a broad brush. The first questioning theme is again heard and like a blast the *presto* comes. It is a whirlwind and the piece ends in storm of scales and octaves. The last bar of the introduction has caused some critical controversy. Gutmann, Mikuli and other Chopin pupils declare for the E flat; Klindworth and Kullak use it. Xaver Scharwenka gives a D natural in the Augener edition. That he is wrong is proved by internal testimony. Chopin intended the E flat, and twenty-eight bars later employs a similar effect; indeed, the entire composition **contains** examples—look at the first bar of the Waltz episode. As Niecks puts it, "this dissonant E flat may be said to be the emotional keynote of the whole poem. It is a questioning thought that like a sudden pain shoots through mind and body." There is still more confirmatory evidence. Mr. Ferdinand von Inten, a well-known pianist and pedagogue of New York, saw the original Chopin manuscript at Stuttgart. It was the property of Professor Lebert; and it contains the much discussed E flat. This testimony ought to be final; besides, the D natural robs the bar of its meaning and is insipid. On the third page, third bar, Kullak uses F natural in the treble; so does Klindworth, though F sharp may be found in some editions. On the last page, second bar, first line, Kullak writes the passage beginning in E flat in eighth notes, Klindworth in sixteenths. The close, as Schumann says, "would inspire a poet to write words to it."

How difficult it is not to speak of Chopin except in terms of impressioned prose. Louis Ehlert, classicist by profession, but a romantic in feeling, wrote of the second Ballade: "Perhaps the most touching of all that Chopin has written is the tale of the F major Ballade. I have witnessed children lay aside their games to listen thereto. It appears like some fairy-tale that has become music. The four-voiced part has such a clearness withal, it seems as if warm spring breezes were waving the little leaves of the palm trees. How soft and sweet a breath steals over the senses and the heart!" This Ballade, though dedicated to Robert Schumann, did not excite his warmest praise. "A less artistic work than the first," he wrote, "but equally fantastic and intellectual. Its impassioned episodes seem to have been inserted afterward. I remember very well that when Chopin played this Ballade for me it finished in F major; it now closes in A minor." However, Chopin's musical instinct was seldom at fault, an ending in the major would have hurt this tone-poem, written, as the composer says, under the direct inspiration of Mickiewicz's "Le Lac des Willis." Niecks does not accept Schumann's dictum as to the supposed inferiority of this second Ballade. He is quite justified in asking how "two such wholly dissimilar things can be weighed in this fashion." In truth they cannot. "The second Ballade possesses beauties in no way inferior to those of the first," he continues. "What can be finer than the simple strains of the opening section! They sound as if they had been drawn from the people's store-house of song. The entrance of the *presto* surprises, and seems out of keeping with what precedes; but what we hear after the return of the *tempo primo*—the development of those strains, or rather the cogitations on them—justifies the presence of the *presto*. The second appearance of the latter leads to an urging, restless *coda* in A minor, which closes in the same key and *pianissimo* with a few bars of the simple, serene, now veiled

first strain." Rubinstein bore great love for this second Ballade. This is what is meant for him: "Is it possible that the interpreter does not feel the necessity of representing to his audience—a field flower caught by a rush of wind, a caressing of the flower by the wind; the resistance of the flower, the stormy struggle of the wind; the entreaty of the flower, which at last lies there broken; and paraphrased—the field flower a rustic maiden, the wind a knight."

I can find "no lack of affinity" between the *andantino* and *presto*. The surprise is dramatic, withal rudely vigorous. Chopin's robust treatment of the first theme results in a strong piece of craftsmanship. The episodical nature of this Ballade is the fruit of the esoteric moods of the composer. It follows a hidden story, and has the quality—as has also the second Impromptu—of great, unpremeditated art. It shocks one by its abrupt, but by no means fantastic, transitions. The key-color is changeful, and the fluctuating themes are well contrasted. It was written at Majorca when the composer was only too noticeably disturbed in body and soul. *Presto con fuoco* Chopin marks the second section. Like Klindworth, Kullak prefers the E nine bars before the return of the *presto*. At the eighth bar, after this return, Kullak adheres to the E, instead of F at the beginning of the bar, treble clef. Klindworth indicates both. Nor does Kullak follow Mikuli in using a D in the *coda*; he prefers D sharp instead of a natural. I wish this Ballade were oftener heard in public. It is almost neglected for the third in A flat, which, as Ehlert says, has the voice of the people.

The third Ballade, once known as the "Undine," after the poem of Mickiewicz, is the schoolgirl's delight, who familiarly toys with its demon, seeing only favor and prettiness in its elegant measures. In it "the refined, gifted Pole, who is accustomed to move in the most distinguished circles of the French capital, is preëminently to be recognized," remarks Schumann. Forsooth, it is aristocratic, gay, piquant, graceful, and also something more. Even in its playful moments there is delicate irony, a spiritual sporting with graver and more passionate emotions. Those broken octaves which each time usher in the second theme, with its infectious rhythmic lilt, what an ironically joyous fillip they give to the imagination! "A coquettish grace—if we accept by this expression that half unconscious toying with the power that charms and fires, that follows up confession with reluctance—seems the very essence of Chopin's feeling." Ehlert evidently sees a ball-room picture of brilliancy, with the regulation tender avowal. But the episodes in this Ballade are so attenuated of grosser elements that none but psychic meanings should be read into them. The disputed passage is on the fifth page of the Kullak edition, after the trills. A measure is missing in Kullak, who, like Klindworth, gives it a footnote.

To my mind this repetition adds emphasis, though it is a formal blur. And what an irresistible moment it is, this delectable territory, before the darker mood of the C sharp minor part is reached. Niecks becomes enthusiastic over the insinuation and persuasion of the work, "the composer showing himself in a fundamentally caressing mood." The ease with which the entire composition floats proves that when in mental health Chopin was not daunted by larger forms. There is moonlight in this music, and some sunlight too, but the prevailing moods are coquetry and sweet contentment. Contrapuntal skill is shown in the working-out section. Chopin always wears his learning lightly, it does not oppress us. The inverted dominant pedal in the C sharp minor episode reveals, with the massive *coda*, a great master. Kullak suggests some variants. He uses the transient shake in the third bar, instead of the *appoggiatura* which Klindworth prefers. Klindworth attacks the trill on the second page with the upper tone, A flat. Kullak and Mertke—in the Steingräber edition—are in substantial agreement in the performance of the passage. Mikuli is the most logical.

About the fourth and glorious Ballade in F minor I could write a volume. It is Chopin in his most reflective, yet most lyrical mood. A passionate lyrism is the keynote of the work, with a *nuance* of self-absorption, suppressed feeling—truly Slavic this trait of shyness—and a concentration that is remarkable even for Chopin. The narrative tone is sometimes missing after the first page, a rather moody and melancholy pondering often usurping its place. It is the mood of a man who examines with morbid, curious insistence the malady that devours his soul. This Ballade is the companion to the Fantaisie-Polonaise, and, as a Ballade, "fully worthy of its sisters," to quote Niecks once more. Its theme in F minor has the elusive charm of a very slow, mournful waltz, and returns twice bejewelled,

yet never overladen. Here is the very apotheosis of the ornament; in the figuration the idea is displayed in dazzling relief. There are episodes and transitional passage-work distinguished by novelty and the highest art. At no place is there virtuosity for its own sake. The cadenza in A is a pause for breath, rather a sigh, before the rigorously logical imitations which presage the reëntrance of the theme. How wonderful is the treatment of the Introduction. What a harmonist is Chopin. Consider the scales beginning in D flat for the left hand —how suave, how satisfying is this page. And what could be more evocative of dramatic suspense than the sixteen bars before the mad, terrifying *coda*. How the solemn splendors of the half-notes weave an atmosphere of mystic tragedy. De Lenz in his "Great Piano Virtuosos of our Time" (G. Schirmer)—a book I heartily commend to music students for its sympathetic portraits of Liszt, Chopin, Tausig and Henselt—describes the interpretation of the Ballade at the hands of the mighty Karl Tausig. He mentions a "lingering" in the reading which is the *tempo rubato*, as a rule fatally misunderstood by the majority of Chopin players. De Lenz in a note quotes Meyerbeer—Meyerbeer, who quarrelled with Chopin over the rhythm of a certain Mazurka—as asking: "Can one reduce women to notation? They would breed mischief were they emancipated from the measure."

There is poetic passion in the curves of this most eloquent composition. It is Chopin at the summit of his supreme art, an art alembicated, personal, intoxicating. I know nothing in music like the F minor Ballade, nothing so intimate, so subtly distinctive.

James Huneker

Thematic Index

BALLADES

Première Ballade

Op. 23

Page 3

Deuxième Ballade

Op. 38

Page 18

Troisième Ballade

Op. 47

Page 28

Quatrième Ballade

Op. 52

Page 42

à Mr. le Baron de Stockhausen

Première Ballade

Revised, edited and fingered by
Rafael Joseffy

F. Chopin. Op. 23

* In some editions:
In manchen Ausgaben:

Carl Tausig { played: spielte: }

à Robert Schumann

Deuxième Ballade

Revised, edited and fingered by
Rafael Joseffy

F. Chopin. Op. 38

Presto con fuoco

Presto con fuoco

à Mlle de Noailles

Troisième Ballade

Revised, edited and fingered by
Rafael Joseffy

F. Chopin. Op. 47

* In the Kullak Edition:
* In der Kullak-Ausgabe:

à Mme la Baronne C. de Rothschild

Quatrième Ballade

Revised, edited and fingered by
Rafael Joseffy

F. Chopin. Op. 52

The upper fingering, without the 3d finger, is for small hands.
*) Der obere Fingersatz, ohne den 3ten finger, für kleinere Hände.

Or:
Oder:

Or, as facilitated:
Oder zur Erleichterung: